Farm Animals in Spanish: (Animals de Granja) Dot Markers Activity Book

Merry Pancakes Publishing

TIPS:

1. Place a piece of paper or cardboard under the page to avoid any color bleeding through
2. Once done, cut each page out and hang up

Want free extra pages?

Send us an email at merrypancakespublishing@gmail.com with the subject "Farm Animals Spanish Dot Markers Book"

This book belongs to:

_____

_____

_____

VOCABULARY

RABBIT = CONEJO
CHICK = POLLITO
CHICKEN = POLLO
COW = VACA
DOG = PERRO
DONKEY = BURRO
DUCK = PATO
GOAT = CABRO
GOOSE = GANSO
HEN = GALLINA
HORSE = CABALLO
MALLARD DUCK = PATO MALLARD
PIG = CERDO
RAM = CARNERO
ROOSTER = GALLO
SHEEP = OVEJA
TURKEY = PAVO

CONEJO

VACA

CABRO

POLLO

CERDO

CARNERO

POLLO

PATO

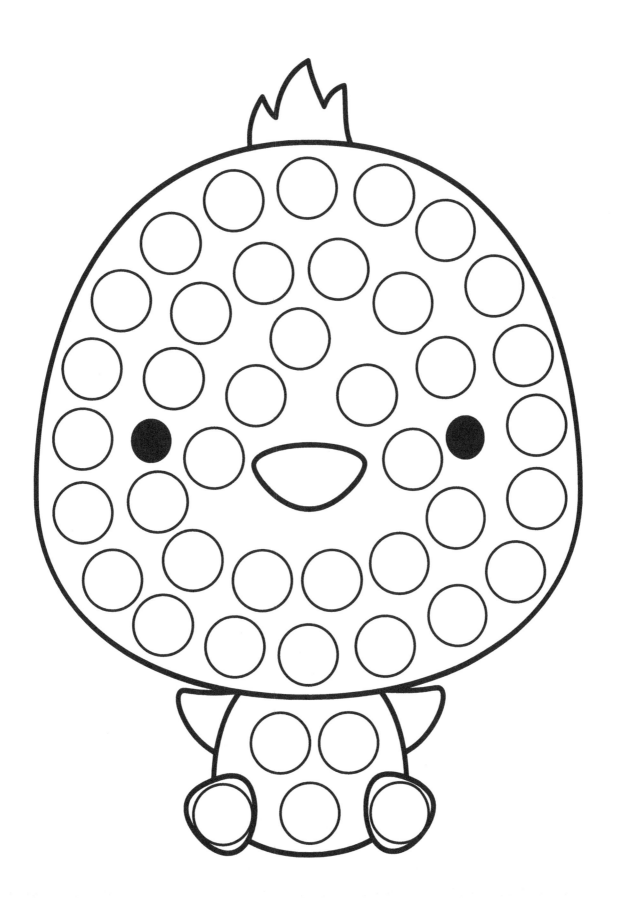

OVEJA

CABALLO

CONEJO

PERRO

POLLITOS

PATO

OVEJA

PAVO

VACA

GALLO

OVEJA

PATO

CABALLO

CABRO

OVEJA

POLLO

CERDO

VACA

POLLITO

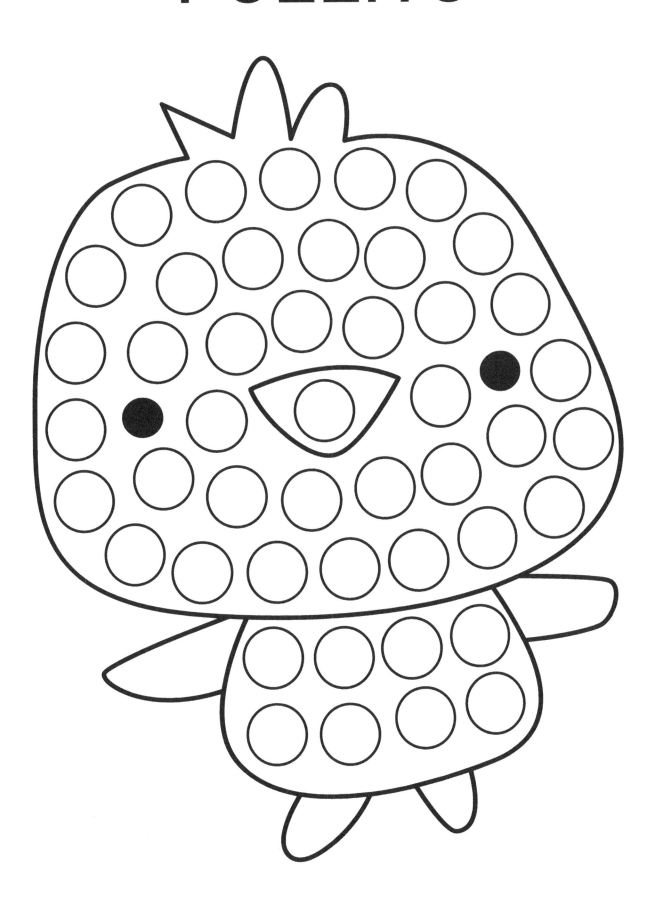

CARNERO

OVEJA

BURRO

CERDO

CABRO

VACA

PATO

CABALLO

POLLO

OVEJA

GALLO

CABRO

CERDO

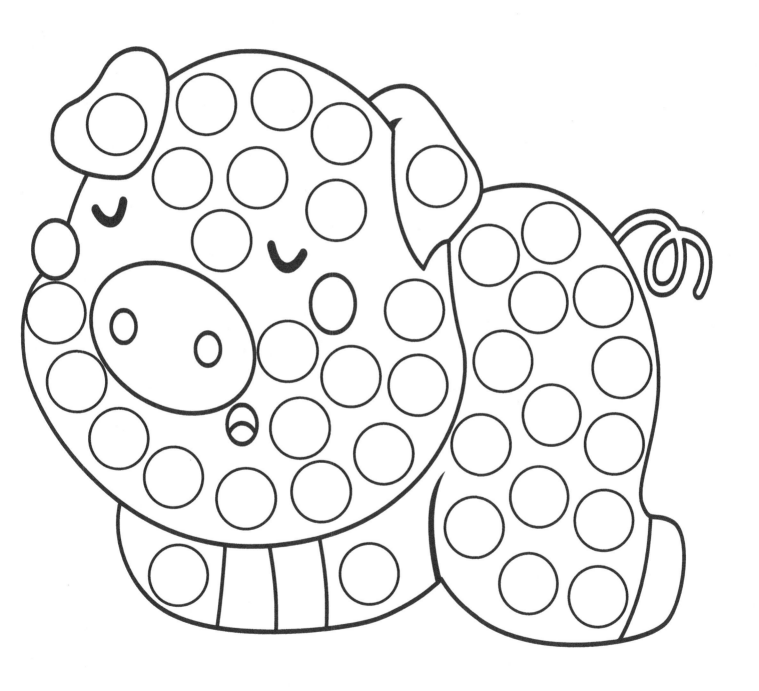

PATO

CERDO

PAVO

GALLINA

VACA

GALLO

POLLITO

GANSO

POLLITO

PATO MALLARD

CERDO

GALLINA

Made in the USA
Las Vegas, NV
18 December 2024